How
the Wind
Blows

How the Wind Blows

KATHERINE D. MARKO

illustrated by **Bettye Beach**

Abingdon

Nashville

HOW THE WIND BLOWS

Library of Congress Cataloging in Publication Data

MARKO, KATHERINE.
  How the wind blows.
  SUMMARY: Describes the various types of winds and
their names in different parts of the world and discusses
both the destructive and beneficial aspects of wind.
    1. Winds—Juvenile literature.   [1. Winds]
I. Title.
QC931.4.M37   551.5'18   80-22754

ISBN 0-687-17680-8

To the memory of my aunt

Grace Lafferty

whose patience and kindness
were like favoring winds

Air is always around us, even when everything seems still. But when air moves, it becomes wind.

If the wind moves in a soft, swishy way, we call it a breeze. It can touch your face as gently as a falling leaf.

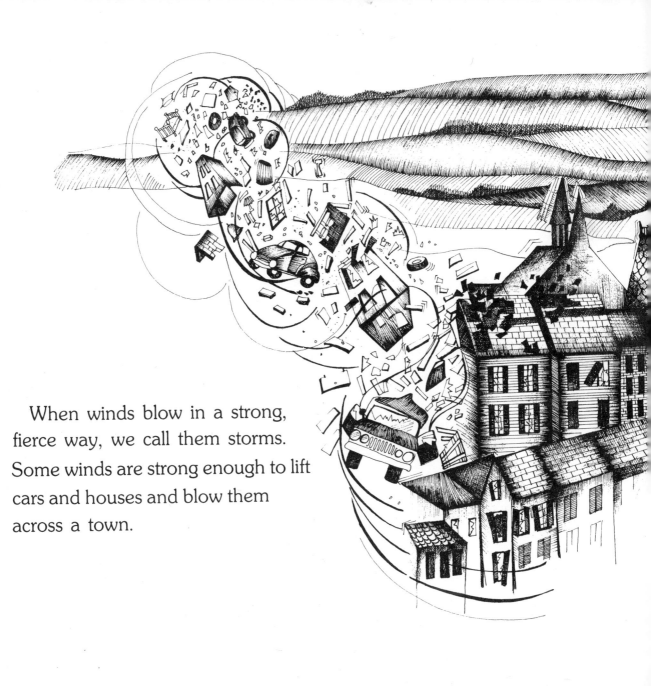

When winds blow in a strong, fierce way, we call them storms. Some winds are strong enough to lift cars and houses and blow them across a town.

Air turns into wind when hot air mixes with cold air, high above the earth. Sometimes this mixture makes the wind much stronger than it is at other times.

That is how storms begin. A mountain or an ocean or flat land can change the wind, too.

The wind often blows from just one direction. It also can toss from every side, making treetops sway and clouds tumble across the sky.

A strong whirling wind that starts to form over the middle of the
Atlantic Ocean is called a hurricane. It blows and spins almost as fast as
a racing car.

When it reaches towns along the shore, it can uproot trees, flatten buildings, and drive the ocean water into the streets.

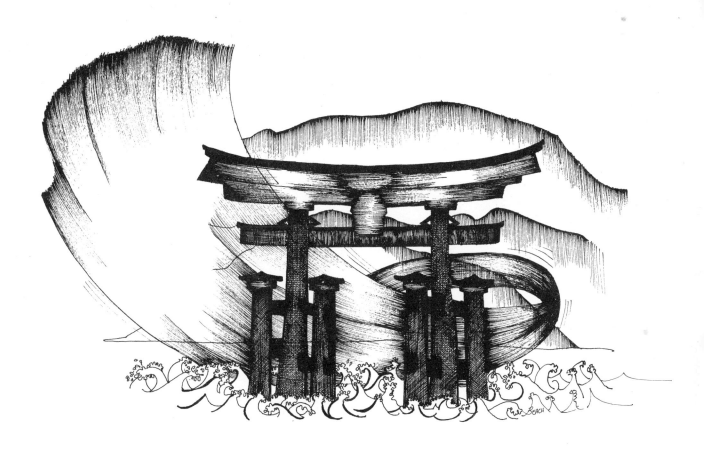

In other places, storms like hurricanes are called by other names. Those in the Pacific Ocean that strike the coasts of China and Japan are called typhoons.

Those that roar into India and East Pakistan are called cyclones.
The people in the Philippine Islands call such storms *baguios*.

And in Australia they are known as "willy-willies." They are all fierce, destructive storms.

A tornado is a violent whirling wind, too. But it blows over land. It spins in a funnel shape and turns dark from sucking up dust and dirt. When it touches the ground, it scoops up or sweeps away everything in its path.

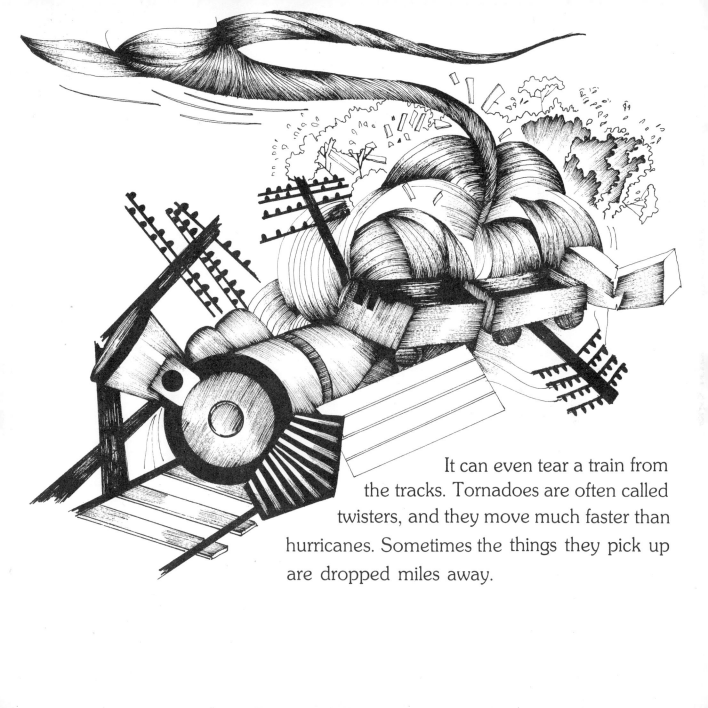

It can even tear a train from the tracks. Tornadoes are often called twisters, and they move much faster than hurricanes. Sometimes the things they pick up are dropped miles away.

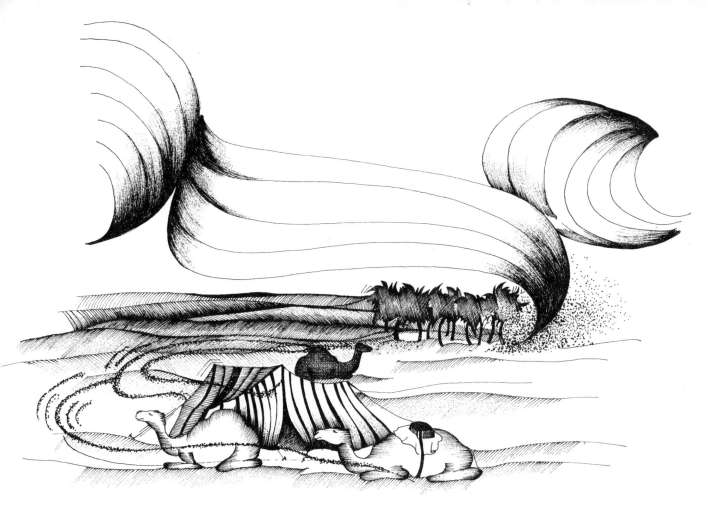

There are many other names for strong winds. There are simooms, which rage over the deserts of Asia and Africa. They cause terrible sand storms.

Monsoons blow in over the coast of India and East Asia. In summer they carry rain, day after day. In Alaska and the most southern part of South America, there are "williwaws." These are violent winds that move down the mountains to the sea.

The "devil wind" is hot and dry. It blows across the desert in Southern California.

There is even a wind called the "snow-eater" that blows down the Rocky Mountain slopes and evaporates the snow along the way.

Storms might make the wind seem like an enemy. But it is a good
friend, too. The wind scatters pollen and seeds from trees and plants.
It carries rain to make the seeds grow.

Sailboats need the wind to puff out their sails and move them across the water. Favorable winds can give you a fine ride in a big hot-air balloon or in a glider.

In many places windmills are used to pump water or to grind grain. The windmill blades are turned by wind power. So windmills can really save other energy, such as gas and electricity.

When the wind is blowing your way, it can carry sounds to you from far away, like a school bell, a train whistle, or a dog's bark.

It carries smells like the
perfume of a rose garden. Or it can
bring you the delicious smell of a
bakery or the fresh smell from
a field of mint.

On a hot day, the wind will cool you off.

The wind also helps animals. It carries the scent of other animals and of humans who might be their enemies.

The wind is helpful and friendly
in many different ways. And how
could anyone fly a kite without the wind!